AXIS

M000200578

A Parent's Guide to Teen FOMO

A Parent's Guide to Influencers

A Parent's Guide to Instagram

A Parent's Guide to TikTok

A Parent's Guide to YouTube

A PARENT'S GUIDE TO

TIKTOK

axis

Tyndale House Publishers
Carol Stream, Illinois

Visit Tyndale online at tyndale.com.

Visit Axis online at axis.org.

Tyndale and Tyndale's quill logo are registered trademarks of Tyndale House Ministries.

A Parent's Guide to TikTok

For information about special discounts for bulk purchases, please contact Tyndale House Publishers at csresponse@tyndale.com, or call 1-855-277-9400.

Library of Congress Cataloging-in-Publication Data

A catalog record for this book is available from the Library of Congress.

ISBN 978-1-4964-6726-3

Printed in the United States of America

28	27	26	25	24	23	22
7	6	5	4	3	2	1

There's huge enticement to get famous, which could encourage kids to do things they wouldn't normally do to get a larger audience.

**FRANNIE UCCIFERRI,
COMMON SENSE MEDIA**

CONTENTS

A LETTER FROM AXIS

Dear Reader,

We're Axis, and since 2007, we've been creating resources to help connect parents, teens, and Jesus in a disconnected world. We're a group of gospel-minded researchers, speakers, and content creators, and we're excited to bring you the best of what we've learned about making meaningful connections with the teens in your life.

This parent's guide is designed to help start a conversation. Our goal is to give you enough knowledge that you're able to ask your teen informed questions about their world. For each guide, we spend weeks reading, researching, and interviewing parents and teens in order to distill everything you need to know about the topic at hand. We encourage you to read the whole thing and then to use the questions we include to get the conversation going with your teen—and then to follow the conversation wherever it leads.

As Douglas Stone, Bruce Patton, and Sheila Heen point out in their book *Difficult Conversations*, "Changes in attitudes and behavior rarely come about because of arguments, facts, and attempts to persuade. How often do *you* change your values and beliefs—or whom you love or what you want in life—based on something someone tells you? And how likely are you to do so when the person who is trying to change you doesn't seem fully aware of the reasons you see things differently in the first place?"[1] For whatever reason, when we believe that others are trying to understand *our* point of view, our defenses usually go down, and we're more willing to listen to *their* point of view. The rising generation is no exception.

So we encourage you to ask questions, to listen, and then to share your heart with your teen. As we often say at Axis, discipleship happens where conversation happens.

Sincerely,
Your friends at Axis

---

[1] Douglas Stone, Bruce Patton, and Sheila Heen, *Difficult Conversations: How to Discuss What Matters Most*, rev. ed. (New York: Penguin Books, 2010), 137.

FOR GEN Z, TIKTOK IS THE APP TO BEAT

TIKTOK (FORMERLY MUSICAL.LY) has rapidly gained popularity among teens and tweens since its launch in 2016. As a "destination for short-form mobile video,"[1] users upload videos of themselves lip-syncing, telling jokes, dancing, etc.

For parents of teens and tweens who use the app (or keep asking to), it's helpful to know what it is, its pitfalls and dangers, and how to talk to them about it in order to help them pursue health in every area of their lives.

WHAT IS TIKTOK, AND HOW POPULAR IS IT?

TO FULLY UNDERSTAND TIKTOK and its appeal, we need to go back to its origins as Musical.ly. Musical.ly was a mobile app for making fifteen-second lip-syncing videos that launched in the US in 2014 and quickly grew in popularity to 200 million registered users.[2] It even partnered with NBC for the 2018 Winter Olympics to give its users special behind-the-scenes footage. Within the first weekend of the Olympics, Musical.ly had produced over 10 million engagements.[3]

It was reminiscent of the now-defunct Vine (which made somewhat of a comeback with Byte[4]), a social media platform where users could share six-second-long videos (which could be amusing and clever and led to fame for a number of Viners, one notable example being pop star Shawn Mendes[5]). Because of this,

Musical.ly filled a hole for many Viners, as well as offering some new features.

According to the *Wall Street Journal*, "Musical.ly's great innovation was making the video *selfie* a thing."[6] Musical.ly videos could be up to fifteen seconds long, and users were able to add music to them, choosing from numerous songs in the app's database or from their own libraries. It was easy for users to creatively edit the videos by adding various effects. They could then share their creations either publicly or privately.

Musical.ly gave rise to quite a few teen stars in its own right. Famous users include Baby Ariel, Jacob Sartorius, and twins Lena and Lisa Mantler. But all of that ended when ByteDance, the Chinese parent company of TikTok (aka "Douyin" in China) that purchased Musical.ly in November 2017,[7] decided to absorb Musical.ly into TikTok in August 2018. The Musical.ly app was no more, and users' accounts were migrated over to the highly similar TikTok app.

Now that TikTok has been combined with Musical.ly's existing user base, ByteDance claims it has over 1 billion active users in 155 countries (as of 2021).[8] Many wondered if the merge would turn off Musical.ly lovers, but the data seems to show the opposite. In the iOS app store, TikTok maintains a 4.8 out of 5 stars rating,[9] with over 3.3 billion downloads. It was one of the most-downloaded apps of 2021 across both Android and Apple devices.[10]

TikTok's requirements limit use of the app to anyone thirteen and older, though there's plenty of evidence that many Musical.ly users were quite young (nine years old or even younger),[11] so it's probably true that TikTok has similar demographics. And while there's plenty of anecdotal evidence to support claims that its main user base is thirteen to eighteen years old, specific statistics are hard to find.[12]

HOW DOES IT WORK?

TIKTOK'S MAIN features[13] (which will all be discussed more below) are:

- Video creation: Create, edit, and post videos.

- Effects: Apply filters and other Snapchat-like effects to videos.

- Messaging: Have text-message-style conversations with others.

- Video viewing: Watch others' videos, and like, comment on, or share them.

- Profile viewing: View others' profiles, which consist of a profile pic, following/follower stats, and a feed of their posts.

- Livestreaming: Stream videos in real time.

A lot of teens use TikTok to post videos of themselves lip-syncing and/or dancing to their favorite songs (that's how Baby Ariel got started). Some sing or play instruments along with another song. Some create comedic skits, while others make DIY (do-it-yourself) videos with music in the background. Many make videos and duets to participate in a trend or meme. Check out a list of all the types of video content found on TikTok at https://slate .com/technology/2018/09/tiktok-app -musically-guide.html.

WHAT HAPPENS WHEN I DOWNLOAD TIKTOK?

WHEN WE DOWNLOADED THE APP, it opened with a screen to either accept or decline their terms of service. Once we accepted, it immediately opened with the Home feed of videos from real users (first image), over which were tips for how to use the interface. We did not have to create an account or profile to begin viewing videos. However, in order to follow others or create our own videos, the app prompted us to sign up using a phone number, email address, Apple ID, or a Facebook/Google/Twitter/Instagram account.

We did not have to create an account or profile to begin viewing videos.

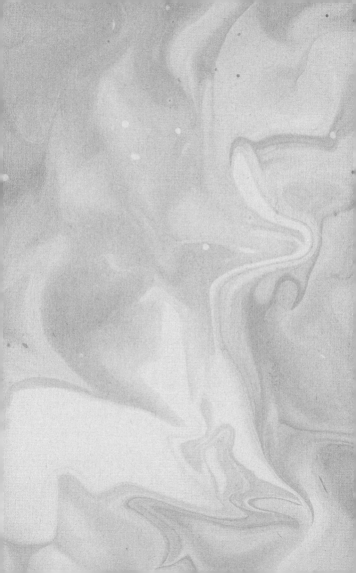

WHAT HAPPENS WHEN I CREATE AN ACCOUNT?

AFTER YOU CHOOSE how you want to sign up, the app asks for your birthday (which isn't ever shown to others). Then it asks you to create a password, after which it verifies that you're not a bot. It will also prompt you to find Facebook friends who are on TikTok, though you can skip this option.

Once you've created your account, you can follow other accounts, have direct message (DM) conversations with other users, customize your profile, and post videos.

Be aware that when you first sign up, your account is public by default. We got a handful of new followers just from posting one video with no hashtags. Also note that, once made public, you cannot delete videos from TikTok's servers. If you publish videos as public and then make your account private, those videos won't be deleted if you uninstall the app.

HOW DO I CREATE A VIDEO?

TAP ON THE PLUS SIGN in the middle of the bottom of the screen to create a video. (You'll have to enable access to the microphone and the camera to do so.) You can choose music for the video right off the bat by tapping "Sounds" at the top middle of the screen, which will bring up the music library sorted by themes. There's also the option to shoot a video first and add music afterward.

OPTIONS WHEN POSTING (MAINLY LOCATED ON RIGHT SIDE OF SCREEN):

- Toggle between the front-facing camera and the back camera

- Choose different recording speeds

- "Beauty," which removes wrinkles, shininess, redness, freckles, etc.

- Instagram-esque filters (created by users)

- Record hands-free

- Turn the flash on or off

- Snapchat-esque effects (created by users)

- Upload a video from the camera roll (which can be longer than sixty seconds)

- Photo templates (choose between different premade templates and upload your own photos)

At the bottom of the screen, you can toggle between fifteen-second, sixty-second, and three-minute videos. To record, simply hold your thumb on the button. When you release, it will stop shooting and allow you to edit that segment, then continue shooting more segments or post it. You can post a video publicly or privately—as well as share to other social media platforms that have already been connected to TikTok—or you can choose to save the video as a Draft. Check out the "Using TikTok" page—at https://support.tiktok.com/en/using-tiktok —for more detailed descriptions of all the app's features.

WHAT'S IN THE HOME FEED?

AS MENTIONED ABOVE, the Home feed (aka the "For You page" or "fyp") is the default tab that appears any time you open the app. It's located in the bottom left corner and shows videos posted by the accounts you're following, as well as videos based on what you have previously liked ("For You"). This screen is a good place to see the accounts/videos your child views when they use the app.

HOW DO I SEARCH FOR SPECIFIC ACCOUNTS OR VIDEOS?

IMMEDIATELY TO THE RIGHT of the Home feed is the Search or Discover tab. By tapping on that, you'll see a new screen that has a search bar across the top, under which is an automatically scrolling carousel of featured or trending accounts and hashtags. Beneath that, it lists trending hashtags with accompanying videos under each one. These hashtags update frequently and encourage users to post videos that have a particular theme, such as #GlowUps or #VibeCheck.

Search results can be filtered by Top, Users, Videos, Sounds, or Hashtags. Simply by selecting one of these categories, the app will populate with what's trending in that category before you ever type anything.

WHERE ARE DIRECT MESSAGES?

YOU CAN ACCESS TIKTOK'S direct message system via the tab second from the right that looks like a chat bubble. This is where you access notifications (like how many people have liked your video) and direct messages. After tapping on the tab, you'll see an icon that looks like a paper airplane in the top right corner. That's where users can speak privately with each other.

If you send a direct message to someone else, the app will tell you that there is a possibility they will not receive the message because of their privacy preferences. If your account is public, you can receive messages from anyone, which is obviously dangerous.

If your account is public,
you can receive messages
from anyone, which is
obviously dangerous.

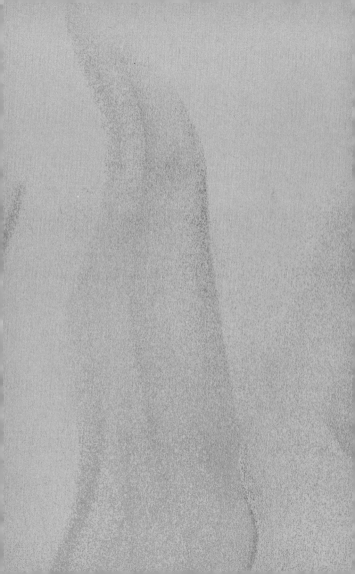

WHAT SHOULD I KNOW ABOUT PROFILES?

YOU CAN ACCESS YOUR PROFILE at the bottom right corner of the app, and there are many options for customizing a profile (left image). You can add a picture, a video, a bio, and links to your Instagram and YouTube pages. You can also share your profile on other social media platforms, such as Facebook and Twitter, and access your QR code to make it easier for others to find your profile.

In others' profiles, you can see every video they have posted, as well as who they're following, who their "fans" are, and how many likes they have gotten (right image).

WHAT'S A DUET?

THIS FEATURE ALLOWS users to collaborate on a video. Users tap the Share button (first image) on any video, then tap on Duet (second image). This will bring up a screen with the original video on one side and a space for the second user to create their corresponding video. Whatever music is in the first video is the music that will be on the duet. If users want to plan a duet ahead of time, they'll use direct messages to coordinate.

CAN USERS LIVESTREAM?

YES AND NO. When we first signed up, we had two notifications about accounts that were currently livestreaming—that is, users who were streaming videos in real time for other users to watch, like, comment on, and send emojis to. But the feature seemed nonexistent within the interface, so after some digging, we discovered that the official story is that the feature only becomes available once a user has reached 1,000 fans, and they need to be at least sixteen to livestream.[14] However, viewing comments on YouTube tutorials for how to go live on TikTok reveals that the feature seems to randomly show up on different accounts. Some reported having the ability to go live despite having very few fans, while others with many fans complained that the feature did not appear for them. It remains to be seen if the company will make this more widely available or tighten down on restrictions.

Whether or not your account has the ability to livestream, it always has the ability to view others' livestreams. When watching a livestream, you not only view the video, but you also see emojis and comments appear on the screen as they're sent.

Users livestream for various purposes. Many users feature their fans on the stream in exchange for the "love" they show (i.e., follows, likes, and emojis).

We saw one user showing off his drumming skills and another doing a Q&A session. One account was livestreaming a photo shoot in a mansion. Several seemed to be active vloggers (video bloggers), and they were using TikTok to promote their Instagram and YouTube channels.

Several characteristics that stood out to us about TikTok's livestreams were:

1. We had instant access to anyone, anywhere in the world. We saw multiple livestreams in foreign languages, such as German and Spanish.

2. People seemed more than willing to spend money to send emojis to their favorite users.

3. It was easy to run across inappropriate content.

4. Many users (mainly those whom the livestreamers were thanking and featuring in their feeds) looked like they were eight or nine years old.

We had instant access
to anyone, anywhere
in the world.

WHY IS MY KID ASKING TO SPEND MONEY ON IT?

YOU'RE PROBABLY FAMILIAR with sending emojis in a text message or email. On TikTok, users can send emojis to other users, but they're not free. They include things like "love bang," "Italian hand," and "panda." You pay for them by going to your profile and tapping the three dots in the upper right corner to access Settings. Once there, tap on Balance. From this screen, you can tap on Recharge (also accessible via the emoji screen at the bottom of a livestream) to purchase coins, which range in price from $0.99 for 100 coins to $99.99 for 10,000. The emojis themselves vary in price, with some of the most expensive ones being "I'm very rich" (1,000 coins or $10) and "drama queen" (5,000 coins or $50).

In one livestream, a fan who sent an "I'm very rich" emoji received two bonus entries in a raffle. In other cases, users who were livestreaming would at least call out and thank the followers who gave generously.

ARE THERE PARENTAL CONTROLS?

AS LONG AS A USER HAS ACCESS to their account, they can make their account public, direct message anyone, and view any videos. But TikTok does offer Family Pairing,[15] which allows parents to remotely disable DMs, set time limits, and enable content restrictions, rather than having to do everything from their kids' devices. The catch: parents must have their own TikTok accounts (boosting TikTok's numbers), and their kids must allow them to link the accounts to each other (a privilege they can revoke at any time). But it's worth being on any app your children are on anyway in order to keep an eye on things and understand what they're experiencing. If you have kids on the app, make sure to enable the feature right away.

TikTok also offers a feature called Digital Well-Being (image), which is accessed via Settings. It offers a Restricted Mode (which uses an algorithm to attempt to limit videos that may not be appropriate for all audiences) and Screen Time Management (which limits the user to no more than two hours on the app per day). Both of these are protected by a passcode (different from the account password), meaning a parent can set the passcode and not give it to the child.

A caveat, though: if a child gets annoyed by this and hasn't really built up their account, they can easily just log out of the account and create a new one without their parents knowing. This is why it's important not to simply put strict boundaries on a phone without talking about them with your teen first. We highly recommend Axis's digital resources *A Parent's Guide to Smartphones*, *A Parent's Guide to iOS*, *A Parent's Guide to Android*, and *A Parent's Guide to Internet Filtering & Monitoring* for more on this perspective. Check out axis.org for more information on these resources.

It's worth being on
any app your children
are on anyway in order
to keep an eye on things
and understand what
they're experiencing.

WHY DO KIDS LOVE IT?

ONE REASON WHY teens and preteens like TikTok is the chance to get famous or, at the very least, to get other people's attention. It's also worth mentioning that users do get money when fans give them emojis, and some influencers reportedly earn millions of dollars per year through brand partnerships and gifts (emojis).[16] So some teens might be enticed by the prospect of making fun videos into a job, rather than having to go to college and/or get a "real" job someday. For example, mega-famous TikTokker and YouTuber Emma Chamberlain doesn't plan to go to college because she's already accomplished so much simply through her social media presence: she's an entrepreneur, content creator, and podcast host, to name a few of her job titles.[17]

Predictably, part of the allure of TikTok is peer pressure. A lot of kids want to be on the app because their friends are on it and because they want to watch popular TikTok personalities. They don't want to be the only one who doesn't know what everyone's talking about.

Teenagers nowadays also enjoy watching people do various activities online. An example of this is YouTube star PewDiePie, who's gained a massive following by posting videos of himself playing video games (which is also a type of video content found on TikTok).

The best way to find out why your kids use (or want to use) TikTok is simply to ask them. That will help you to best understand the underlying drives and needs it fulfills for them, as well as how to plan conversations about the app.

So some teens might be enticed by the prospect of making fun videos into a job, rather than having to go to college and/or get a "real" job someday.

WHAT ARE ITS DANGERS?

THE PRIMARY DANGERS involved with TikTok have to do with how easy it is to view mature content, how easy it can be to connect with online predators, and the potential for cyberbullying.

We don't want to be fearmongers, but we do think it's important to mention some of the harm people have experienced through Musical.ly and now TikTok. One dad in Idaho Falls caught his eleven-year-old daughter sending pictures of herself in her underwear to men who had been asking her for inappropriate videos.[18] Another eleven-year-old girl received rape threats and other sexually graphic messages.[19] In her case, her account was private, and she got those messages after accepting a request from a stranger who she thought was someone she knew. Perhaps saddest of all is the story of a ten-year-old girl in Aurora,

The primary dangers involved with TikTok have to do with how easy it is to view mature content, how easy it can be to connect with online predators, and the potential for cyberbullying.

CO, who committed suicide after someone recorded a fight she was in at school
and posted it on Musical.ly.[20]

These are horror stories that describe
some worst-case scenarios. But what
was our experience with TikTok? The
majority of the videos we saw could be
described as "fluff." Most weren't offen-
sive, nor were they particularly clever.
They were videos of kids lip-syncing to
songs or acting out scenes and trying to
be funny. Something that seems clear is
that many people who use TikTok want
attention and validation.

While TikTok won't allow certain searches,
such as for "sex" or "porn," one of the first
accounts that was recommended to us
as soon as we signed up was highly
inappropriate.

We also saw a girl who was livestreaming and swearing at her users. She used the f-word frequently, as did some of the people commenting in the chat. Other responses to her video were "she is bi" and "r u a girl," to which she responded derisively, "There's more than one gender."

One particularly disturbing trend is the "boyfriend porn check" (watch at your own discretion) most popular in February and March of 2020. Here's how it works: a girl plays a tune that's used in porn videos (each TikTok uses the same tune), and the idea is that if your boyfriend smiles at the song, he watches porn. And of course, this is all filmed for a "funny" video and posted to TikTok for the whole world to see. Another popular trend from March and April of 2020 was the "surprising my boyfriend naked" challenge (watch at your own discretion), in which women record their boyfriend's (or husband's) reaction to their naked bodies. The videos never actually show any nudity, but the towel dropping and reaction reveals enough for the imagination.

The takeaway here is that, though trends like the "boyfriend porn check" and "surprising my boyfriend naked" will fade in popularity, other trends will take their place, and it's impossible to screen them all or keep young social media users from seeing them. This makes regular conversations about TikTok even more necessary.

It's impossible to mention all the things that might be considered dangerous on TikTok. But know that the majority of the content we saw was not graphic. We encountered plenty of videos that were innocuous, many that were boring, and several that showed some talent. But the graphic content we did stumble on was pretty easy to find (not to mention all of the songs that are available with explicit lyrics).

WHAT'S TIKTOK'S POSITION ON MATURE CONTENT?

AMONG OTHER THINGS, TikTok's community guidelines prohibit obscene, pornographic, and abusive content.[21] But similar to platforms such as Instagram and YouTube, TikTok relies on its users to regulate and report any inappropriate content they find, meaning there is always some out there.

To be fair to the app's creators, TikTok states that it is not intended for kids under 13 and strongly encourages parents to be proactive about their children's use of the app: "Hosting candid family conversations about the ways in which your teen engages online, including and beyond TikTok, will help bolster their sense of digital citizenship and empower them to be mindful of their own safety on the internet."[22] The site also lists several resources to help parents encourage their teens to use the app wisely.

While it's sad and shocking to see so many young children finding their worth on TikTok, parents do bear the burden of responsibility for allowing their kids to be on the app. But at the same time, it's hard not to wonder why the app's creators aren't more vigilant about enforcing their own rules.

"Hosting candid family conversations about the ways in which your teen engages online, including and beyond TikTok, will help bolster their sense of digital citizenship and empower them to be mindful of their own safety on the internet."

—TIKTOK

WHAT CAN I DO TO PROTECT MY KIDS?

SO WHAT can we actually do to protect our kids if they're on TikTok?

- Make their accounts private.

- Make sure they don't accept requests from anyone they don't know.

- Block certain accounts if needed.

- Report inappropriate content immediately.[23]

- Share their accounts with them.

- Utilize the features available through Family Sharing and Digital Well-Being.

- Have conversations with them about online safety, identity, worth, value, etc.

- Continue having conversations with them about online safety and their use of TikTok.

You'll notice that these measures only go so far. The girl we mentioned earlier who saw sexually explicit content and received threats thought she was accepting a follow request from someone she knew. And a lot of these steps are ones you would take after your child has already encountered explicit content. One mom, Anastasia Basil, recounts some of the gut-wrenching things she saw on the app and even goes so far as to say that porn is not the worst thing on it. Read her article at https://humanparts.medium.com/porn -is-not-the-worst-thing-on-musical-ly -5df07ab842af/.

As with anything, it's up to you to take into account your children's ages, personalities, and maturity levels when deciding whether or not they can handle TikTok. Because of the easy access to mature content, we recommend that parents don't allow children under age thirteen to use the app, and it might even be better to wait until they're older (Common Sense Media recommends sixteen years old).

Below are some suggestions for questions to ask your kids if you're considering allowing them to use TikTok, as well as if you are already allowing them to use it.

It's up to you to take into account your children's ages, personalities, and maturity levels when deciding whether or not they can handle TikTok.

DISCUSSION QUESTIONS BEFORE GETTING TIKTOK

1. Why do you want to use TikTok? What do you plan to do on the app?

2. How do your friends use TikTok?

3. What are ways you can use the app creatively?

4. Do you think the app will help you have better community? Why or why not?

5. Do you know the dangers of using TikTok?

6. How are you going to protect yourself while using the app?

7. How are you going to keep yourself accountable for the way you use it?

8. Do you think it's worth continuing to use TikTok if you accidentally come across graphic content? Why or why not?

9. Why do you think people are willing to spend a good chunk of money sending emojis to strangers? Would you do this yourself?

DISCUSSION QUESTIONS AFTER GETTING TIKTOK

1. What has stood out to you about TikTok since you started using it?

2. Do you think most people on the app are using it creatively and for good purposes? What do you think motivates other people to use TikTok?

3. Have you come across any mature/ explicit content?

4. Do you think TikTok is deepening your community or isolating you?

5. What do you think about how much time you're spending on TikTok?

6. How is TikTok affecting you, both positively and negatively? How can I help you to better manage the negative effects?

7. What would have to happen for
   you to decide not to be on the app?
   Will you tell me right away if that
   scenario occurs?

8. What do you think about how hard
   others are trying to gain followers
   and views? Do you want those things
   too? What do you think about that
   desire?

ONE LAST THING . . .

WE FOUND THIS SUGGESTION from mom Anastasia Basil (the one who thinks porn isn't the worst thing on the app) an interesting idea worth considering: We parents tell our children that if they stay off all social media—yes, ALL social media, so no Snapchat, Facebook, Instagram, TikTok, and so on—until they're sixteen, they will each get a check for $1,600 to spend however they want. Crazy, but also fascinating. We reward our kids for so many other achievements, so why not, as Basil says, reward them for "winning at peer pressure"?[24] Or, at the very least, perhaps that idea can inspire us to come up with more creative ways of helping our kids have healthy relationships with their phones and social media, rather than simply being the "evil" parents who always say no to the things that seem so important to them.

TAKEAWAYS

IT'S HELPFUL TO REMEMBER that TikTok is a product of two good desires God gave us: to create and to be in community—and it actually is pretty fun to make TikTok videos.

Besides the adult content on the app, the main problem is that there's a huge temptation to get attention in the form of fans, comments, and likes. Growing your fan base is much easier to do when your account is public than when it is private. And a public account comes with a lot of dangers, especially for children. As Basil puts it:

> If your child does not maintain an online self, chances are her social circle is small—friends from school, neighbors, family. If she has a rough day at school, a bell sets her free each afternoon. The jerks who taunted her at lunch

aren't coming home with her for the night. She has space to think, to be with you, to read, to hug her dog, to recover, to get brave. Online, there is no school bell, there is no escape; she exists globally, and so do her mistakes. The ridicule is permanent.[25]

If you decide to let your kids use TikTok, have consistent conversations with them about it. Make sure they're educated on the dangers of connecting with strangers online and that they have accountability.

And don't forget to pray, which is always the most important step you can take and the easiest one to neglect. You can't control your teens or protect them from every peril, but God will always know what's going on in their lives. Rely on Him first and foremost.

TikTok is a product of two good desires God gave us: to create and to be in community.

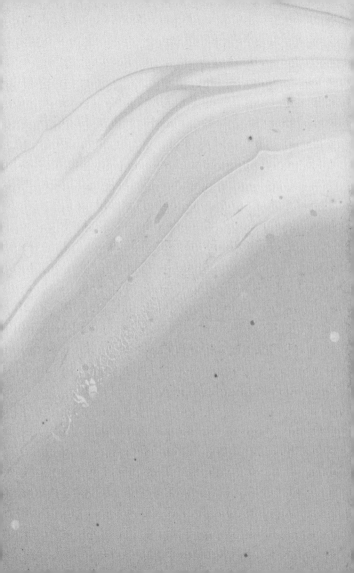

RECAP

- TikTok is quickly growing in popularity with tweens and teens.

- It's fun and quirky because users make fifteen-second or sixty-second videos, have the ability to add music, text, and filters, and are able to create "duets" with other TikTokkers.

- Limited parental controls are available through Family Sharing and Digital Well-Being, but nothing beats constant parental awareness and monitoring.

- As with most other social media apps, it's possible (and easy) for complete strangers to contact users, and it's possible to encounter predators on the platform.

- Many "challenges" originate on TikTok, and they can be anywhere from ridiculous and fun to graphic or even dangerous.

- We never recommend that anyone under the age of thirteen get on TikTok or any other social media platform. Their terms require users to be thirteen or older.

- Users can spend money on the app by purchasing coins to send emoji gifts to other users.

- If you let your kids get TikTok accounts, have regular conversations about the app, how it's affecting them, things they've seen, amount of time spent using it, and more.

If you let your kids get TikTok accounts, have regular conversations about the app, how it's affecting them, things they've seen, amount of time spent using it, and more.

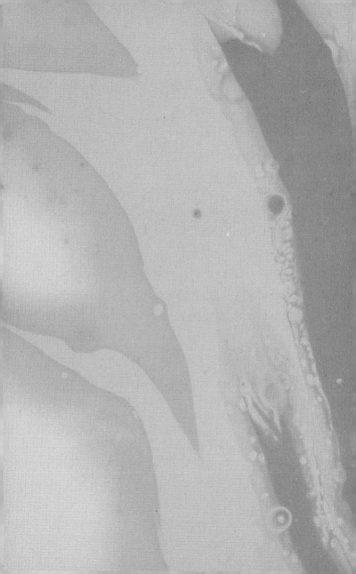

ADDITIONAL RESOURCES

1. "TikTok Parental Guide," https:// newsroom.tiktok.com/en-us /tiktok-parental-guide

2. "TikTok's Top 10 Tips for Parents," https://newsroom.tiktok.com/en-us /tiktoks-top-10-tips-for-parents

3. "What Is TikTok? And Is It Safe? A Guide for Clueless Parents," NBC News, https://www.nbcnews.com /better/lifestyle/what-tiktok-guide -clueless-parents-ncna1066466

4. "TikTok/Musical.ly Guide," Stay Hipp, https://stayhipp.com/apps/stayhipps -tik-tok-musical-ly-guide/

5. "How to Record a Music Video with TikTok," WikiHow (includes screenshots), https://www.wikihow .com/Record-a-Music-Video-with -TikTok

6. "More Younger Members of Generation Z Use TikTok than Facebook," Axios, https://www.axios.com/tiktok-facebook-generation-z-use-a414a30b-4184-415e-9945-949b59727d17.html

7. "Dad Warns of Popular App after Discovering Disturbing Messages Sent to 7-Year-Old," WGN TV, https://wgntv.com/news/trending/dad-warns-of-popular-app-after-discovering-disturbing-messages-sent-to-7-year-old/

8. "Ten-Year-Old Schoolgirls Traumatised after Vile Paedophile 'Hijacked Their Group Gathering on Popular Musical.ly Video App,'" The Daily Mail, https://www.dailymail.co.uk/news/article-4486748/Brisbane-mother-furious-paedophile-Musical-ly-app.html

9. "The Facts about Online Predators Every Parent Should Know," Common Sense Media, https://www.common sensemedia.org/articles/the-facts -about-online-predators-every -parent-should-know

10. "What is TikTok? Is it Safe?" Protect Young Eyes, https://protectyoung eyes.com/apps/tiktok-parental -controls/

11. Check out axis.org for more resources, including *The Culture Translator*, a free weekly email that offers biblical insight on all things teen-related

NOTES

1. "Our Mission," TikTok, accessed March 13, 2022, https://www.tiktok.com/about?lang=en.

2. Yuyu Chen, "Musical.ly Has Lots of Users, Not Much Ad Traction," Digiday, September 5, 2017, https://digiday.com/marketing/musical -ly-starts-selling-ads/.

3. Robert Williams, "Musical.ly Generates 10M Engagements in First Weekend of Olympics Partnership," Marketing Dive, February 16, 2018, https://www.marketingdive.com/news /musically-generates-10m-engagements-in -first-weekend-of-olympics-partnersh/517276/.

4. Shelby Brown, "Byte vs. TikTok: Which Video App Will Live Up to Vine's Legacy?" CNET, February 7, 2020, https://www.cnet.com/tech /mobile/byte-vs-tiktok-which-video-app-will -live-up-to-vines-legacy/.

5. Ella Cerón, "Shawn Mendes's First Vine Isn't What You'd Expect," *Teen Vogue*, October 27, 2016, https://www.teenvogue.com/story /shawn-mendes-first-vine.

6. Mickey Rapkin, "The Social Media Platform That Has Gen Z Obsessed," *WSJ Magazine*, November 1, 2017, https://www.wsj.com /articles/the-social-media-platform-that-has -gen-z-obsessed-1509586335.

7. Kevin Tran, "Social Video App Musical.ly Acquired for up to $1 Billion," Insider, November 13, 2017, https://www .businessinsider.com/social-video-app -musically-acquired-for-up-to-1-billion -2017-11?r=US&IR=T.

8. Maryam Mohsin, "10 TikTok Statistics That You Need to Know in 2021 [Infographic]," Oberlo, February 16, 2021, https://www.oberlo.com /blog/tiktok-statistics.

9. "TikTok," Apple Store Preview, accessed March 14, 2022, https://apps.apple.com/us/app /tiktok/id835599320.

10. Shanon Roberts, "Top 10 Most Downloaded Apps of 2021 So Far," Cyberclick, March 15, 2021, https://www.cyberclick.net /numericalblogen/top-10-most-downloaded -apps-of-2020-so-far.

11. David G. Allan, "The Risks of Crowdsourcing Kids' Screen Decisions," CNN Health, December 5, 2017, https://www.cnn.com/2017/11/10/health/screen-decisions-go-ask-your-dad/index.html.

12. Julia Gray, "Musical.ly, TikTok, and the Memeification of Music," Stereogum, August 7, 2018, https://www.stereogum.com/2005184/musical-ly-tik-tok-music-as-meme/columns/sounding-board/.

13. Frannie Ucciferri, "Parents' Ultimate Guide to TikTok," Common Sense Media, March 5, 2021, https://www.commonsensemedia.org/articles/parents-ultimate-guide-to-tiktok.

14. Devon Delfino, "How to Go Live on TikTok—and 9 Tips to Create Engaging Live Content," Insider, December 2, 2021, https://www.businessinsider.com/how-to-go-live-on-tiktok.

15. Jeff Collins, "TikTok Introduces Family Pairing," TikTok, April 15, 2020, https://newsroom.tiktok.com/en-us/tiktok-introduces-family-pairing.

16. "How Influencers Make Money on TikTok," TapInfluence, accessed April 24, 2022, https://www.tapinfluence.com/make-money-on-tiktok/.

17. Jessica Chia, "A Look into Emma Chamberlain's Virtual Reality," *Allure*, May 10, 2020, https://www.allure.com/story/emma-chamberlain-june-2020-cover-interview.

18. Natalie Hepworth, "He Caught His Daughter Posting Inappropriate Videos. Now This Father Has a Message for Parents," *East Idaho News*, November 28, 2017, https://www.eastidahonews.com/2017/11/parents-have-you-heard-of-musical-ly-another-social-media-platform-kids-misusing/.

19. "Mom Warns Parents about Dangers of Social Media App Musical.ly," Fox 29 Philadelphia, November 14, 2017, https://www.fox29.com/news/mom-warns-parents-about-dangers-of-social-media-app-musical-ly.

20. Tribune Media Wire, "Child Commits Suicide after Bullying Incident Caught on Camera," CBS 6 News Richmond, November 30, 2017, https://www.wtvr.com/2017/11/30/10-year

-old-commits-suicide-after-alleged-bullying
-incident-caught-on-camera/.

21. "Community Guidelines," TikTok, accessed
    March 13, 2022, https://www.tiktok.com
    /community-guidelines?lang=en.

22. "Guardian's Guide," TikTok, accessed March
    13, 2022, https://www.tiktok.com/safety/en
    /guardians-guide/.

23. "Report a Video," TikTok, accessed March 13,
    2022, https://support.tiktok.com/en/safety-hc
    /report-a-problem/report-a-video.

24. Anastasia Basil, "Porn Is Not the Worst Thing
    on Musical.ly/TikTok," Human Parts, March 5,
    2018, https://humanparts.medium.com
    /porn-is-not-the-worst-thing-on-musical-ly
    -5df07ab842af.

25. Basil, "Porn Is Not the Worst Thing on Musical
    .ly/TikTok."

PARENT'S GUIDES
BY AXIS

It's common to feel lost in your teen's world. These pocket-sized guides are packed with clear explanations of teen culture to equip you to have open conversations with your teen, one tough topic at a time. Look for more parent's guides coming soon!

BUNDLE THESE 5 BOOKS AND SAVE

DISCOVER MORE PARENT'S GUIDES, VIDEOS, AND AUDIOS AT AXIS.ORG